Whatever Happened to Lady Chatterley's Lover?

AF597416

Whatever Happened To Lady Chatterley's Lover?

MARTIN LEVIN

Illustrations by Victor Juhasz

Andrews, McMeel & Parker, *A Universal Press Syndicate Company*
Kansas City • New York

Whatever Happened to Lady Chatterley's Lover? copyright © 1985 by Martin Levin. All rights reserved. Printed in the United States of America. No part of this book may be used or reproduced in any manner whatsoever except in the case of reprints in the context of reviews. For information write Andrews, McMeel & Parker, a Universal Press Syndicate Company, 4400 Johnson Drive, Fairway, Kansas 66205.

Library of Congress Cataloging in Publication Data

Levin, Martin.
Whatever happened to Lady Chatterley's lover?

1. Characters and characteristics in literature—Anecdotes, facetiae, satire, etc. I. Title.
PN169.L4 1985 818'.5402 85-7424
ISBN 0-8362-7960-3

For: DONNA

From: MARTIN

Cast of Characters

Introduction

It's reasonable to want to know the further adventures of fictional characters. That's what makes sequels. Too many popular protagonists have disappeared without a trace. To fill this void—we've sent a fictional investigator to find out whatever happened to some heroes (and villains) who were dear to us.

A number of these expeditions were unsuccessful. We could find no trace of Ben Hur. A rumor that he had operated a used chariot lot on the Appian Way proved groundless. Neither would we find a fruitful lead on the Corsican Brothers, although they have made a recent appearance in a movie. (One informant claimed that the Corsican Brothers had merged with the Brothers Ashkenazi and the Brothers Karamazov to form a transcontinental trucking operation known as the Seven Brothers. But this is iffy.)

When news of this project leaked in the *New York Times Book Review*, we received a flood of helpful suggestions, for which we are grateful. From Ira Wallach we got solutions to a batch of our toughest cases. He personally discovered and described whatever happened to Hester Prynne, Jonathan Livingston Seagull, Anna Karenina, Christopher Robin, Larry (of *The Razor's Edge*), ex-U.S. Air Force Capt. John Yossarian, Aïda and Rhadames, among others. From Robert Aldrich we got a report on the status of Dr. Frankenstein's assistant Igor, Jeeves, et al. John Ferris got through to Leopold Bloom. And from Fred Gurner we received a tip on the whereabouts of Holden Caulfield. Victor Juhasz caught his likeness in pen and ink, since Holden is very camera shy.

Some of these lives took interesting and exciting turns; if others didn't amount to much—we're just giving you the facts.

Martin Levin

Big Brother

(last seen in George Orwell's 1984*)*

Winston Smith underwent aversion therapy by an underground psychotherapist to conquer successfully his rodent phobia. With this behind him, he organized a resistance movement against Big Brother. A guerrilla force of money machine technicians recruited from the staffs of U.S. commercial banks easily knocked out Oceania's entire telemetry. With the terminals "down," Big Brother couldn't watch anything, except a simple read-out: "I'm sorry. This nation is out of order. The nearest operational country is in South America."

Big Brother has been reportedly seen in Paraguay.

George Apley

(last seen in John P. Marquand's The Late George Apley*)*

The obituary of George Apley listed his outside interests as "The Save Boston Association," bird watching and philosophy. But a biography written by his daughter Eleanor ripped to shreds Apley's veneer of Boston Brahmin respectability.

In his home on Beacon Hill, wrote Eleanor, her father kept an extensive wardrobe of women's clothes which he wore everywhere except to the office. He was especially partial to cashmere sweater sets, tweed skirts, and for more formal occasions, a simple black dress from Chanel.

"Father was a transvestite," Eleanor wrote in a memoir entitled *Apley after Hours*, "and he lived in constant fear of his double life being exposed. It made him an alcoholic. Toward the end of his life he was in and out of the detox ward of Mass. General."

If Apley had succeeded in concealing his compulsion for drag and drink, why had his daughter now revealed it?

"That's a good question," Eleanor replied in an interview in the *National Enquirer*. "My feeling was that someone was bound to come along and do an unauthorized biography of Dad. So the biographer might just as well be me."

Paperback rights to *Apley after Hours* have been sold for six figures, and a movie is in the making with Joel Gray in the title role.

STAR
KILLERS

Peter Pan

(last seen in James Barrie's Peter Pan*)*

We found Wendy Darling in a nursing home in Brighton. Wendy must have been ninety if she was a day, but her blue eyes twinkled and she seemed surprisingly nimble. She attributed her good health to a lifetime of flying. "There's nothing better for the circulation," she said. "If everybody could fly," she added, over a cup of tea, "nobody would have aches and pains."

Did she ever see Peter?

"On and off," Wendy said. "But Peter's very depressed. Things have changed too much for him."

She lit a Player's and took a deep drag.

"The disappearance of the nuclear family was a big jolt to Peter and The Lost Boys."

Suddenly, we were joined by a youth in an Ultrasuede suit and matching hat.

"That's right, Wendy," he said. "If *nobody* wants to grow up, where's the fun? Computer games. Videos. Every middle-aged nerd wearing a track suit." He shook his head sadly. "Today, it's all Never Land."

He began to fade and disappeared into a cloud of Wendy's cigarette smoke.

"I told you he was depressed," said Wendy.

Omar the Tentmaker

(last seen in The Rubaiyat of Omar Khayyam*)*

Middle Eastern rumor has it that Omar was a problem drinker. He began leaving out the loaf of bread and the female company and concentrated on the jugs of wine. An old verse found in a camel saddlebag allegedly belonging to Omar gives this credence:

I woke of a sudden in the Bowl of Night.
For in my dreams I'd seen a ghastly sight—
A herd of spectral camels that made me blink,
As every single one of them was shocking pink!

Obviously, Omar was so shook up that even his prosody is not in the familiar vein. In the bazaars, it is said that when Omar gave up drinking, he could no longer write poetry.

Kismet.

Willy Loman

(last seen in Arthur Miller's Death of a Salesman*)*

With the help of a private detective agency, we found Willy Loman living in a luxury condo in Anchorage, Alaska, under an assumed name.

Willy was very old, but in surprisingly good health. He snapped his fingers, and a houseman in a white mess jacket brought in a punch bowl of black caviar surrounded by rounds of melba toast.

"Beluga," said Willy. "I get it direct from Murmansk. Dig in."

"We thought you were dead," we said through a mouthful of caviar.

Willy chuckled. "That was the whole idea. My insurance policy had the usual suicide clause. So if I was going to kill myself for my insurance—I had to make it look good. Which I did. But then I had to disapppear. Never mind how."

"Are you now going public?" we asked.

"Not really," Willy said. "But it doesn't matter. The statute of limitations has run out, so I don't have to hide. I keep in touch. My sons Biff and Happy opened a sporting goods store with the insurance money and made a big success. Now they're into computers. My wife Linda remarried. Why not?" he laughed. "Have some champagne?"

The houseman poured two glasses of Dom Perignon.

"How did you finally make it?" we asked.

"Finally?" Willy said. "I was always a great salesman. Do you know what I sold?" We had to admit we didn't. "Neither did I," Willy said. "That bum Arthur Miller never put it into the play! Listen—anybody who can spend a lifetime selling *nothing* has got to be a great salesman! Right? So I came up to Alaska and went into business with my brother Ben. Plastics. Ben passed away many years ago and the business became mine. Have a cigar." He handed me a box of Partagas. "I have them flown in," he said.

"Do you have a recipe for success?" we asked.

"Yes," said Loman, lighting up. "If you're going to be a salesman, you gotta have merchandise. Otherwise you may end up killing yourself."

The Time Traveller

(last seen in H.G. Wells' The Time Machine*)*

The Time Traveller left London in 1895 and returned in 1985. He did not know that his home had been leveled and a high-rise built in its place, so when the Traveller returned, he misjudged his landing and damaged the Time Machine beyond repair.

The Traveller's clothes excited no comment, even after an eighty-nine year lapse. Everyone thought he was a Teddy Boy. But when he went looking for work, the time lapse in his résumé was a problem.

When he explained to a man at the employment agency that he had been visiting the Eloi and the Worlocks, the man called a security guard and the Traveller had to leave in a hurry.

Finally, the Traveller fed his résumé and his problem into a computer and requested an answer.

The computer's reply was that he should get himself a job in the General Post Office.

"Why?" he asked.

"Because in the Post Office," the answer came back, "time is of no importance."

This the Traveller did. He was immediately hired and could devote his spare time, which is most of the day, to building a new Time Machine.

Scrooge

(last seen in Charles Dickens' A Christmas Carol*)*

Ebenezer Scrooge never reverted to his parsimonious ways. He became open and generous and pursued a lifestyle suitable to his income. He lost half his fortune in bad investments. The other half disappeared when he married a sprightly widow.

When the money was gone, she disappeared too.

Although Bob Cratchit had been saving Scrooge's many Christmas bonuses and other largesse, he bought out Scrooge for a pittance. The old man was really hard up. When the new firm, Cratchit Associates was established, Cratchit allowed Scrooge to stay on as an employee, but only as a "temp"—which meant that he owed him no extra benefits.

Scrooge went to bed every night with a poker in his hand, in case Marley's ghost ever reappeared. It never did, although Scrooge believed he heard him cackling from time to time.

Scrooge died a year later, and on the Christmas that followed his death he appeared as a ghost in Cratchit's bedroom.

"What the dickens are you doing here?" shouted Cratchit at the apparition.

Anna Karenina

(when last heard of, from Leo Tolstoy, she was running into some difficulty with a train)

Contrary to popular belief, Anna Karenina survived her encounter with the train. Although the locomotive was damaged beyond repair, Anna herself clung with amazing tenacity to life and underwent two years of reconstructive surgery before emerging as a reasonable facsimile of herself. For a while she went into seclusion and passed her time sticking pins into a wax effigy called Vronsky.

She was well on in years by the time of the Bolshevik Revolution. Her son, a corporal in the Red army, was promoted to marshal after he denounced his mother for various bourgeois deviations, citing foremost her contributions to the moral degeneracy of the Army Officer Corps. In his denunciation, Anna's son said, "Mother was constantly making invidious comparisons between the pleasures of the flesh and the First Five Year Plan."

Embittered, and facing Siberian exile, Anna escaped by disguising herself as Anna Louise Strong. She made her way to the United States, where she established a Russian émigré colony on the shores of Lake Tahoe. Although well into the second century of her life, she succeeded in attracting a coterie of superannuated Russian naval officers who treated her with as much gallantry as their years permitted. She became a strong and active proponent of the freeze, but she did not want a nuclear freeze. She wanted to freeze the army.

When she lay dying, surrounded by her loyal friends, she smiled wanly and said, "It's a shame that Tolstoy knew so little about the navy."

IRA WALLACH

Mrs. de Winter

(last seen in Daphne Du Maurier's Rebecca*)*

We found Mr. and Mrs. Maxim de Winter at the Hotel Vielle Fontaine in Maison Lafitte, a town near Paris where the main occupation was horse racing. Mrs. de Winter met us in the hotel garden. A tea table was set for two. "Sorry Max couldn't be here," she said. "He's at an auction of two-year-olds. Horses have been his passion, you know, after he gave up boating."

She filled us in on what had happened since Manderley. "I'd been living on a pink cloud," she said. "Maybe a trifle too pink." She poured two cups of tea and offered us a watercress sandwich. "I mean, romance is wonderful but it's not everything. My eyes were opened by one of you Americans. Betty Friedan. An inspiration. After *The Feminine Mystique*, I decided to resume my maiden name. But it was impossible." A frown flitted across her classic features.

"The problem was, I had no maiden name. That damned Du Maurier never gave me one. I am nameless, except for Mrs. de Winter. It's been such an embarrassment at consciousness-raising meetings." She took a thoughtful sip of tea. "So what I've done is to refer to myself as Ms. de Winter. It's better than nothing. And Max has been very understanding.

"Basically, my trouble has always been a poor self-image. That bitch Danvers intimidated me with her power dressing—those chatelaine keys and all. But that's all in the past."

What about Manderley? "Loved the place," said Ms. de Winter. "But rebuilding was out of the question. The cost of a sprinkler system alone would have been astronomical."

Ye
IRS

Robin Hood

(last seen in The Adventures of Robin Hood. *Author unknown)*

Legend has it that Robin Hood died when he was bled to death by his cousin, a treacherous prioress, who was treating him for a cold.

This was actually a cover story concocted by Robin himself.

The true story is that the king gave up sending the sheriff after Robin Hood and instead sent the tax collector.

To avoid imprisonment for tax evasion, Robin Hood assumed the identity of Friar Tuck, who was tax exempt. Friar Tuck assumed the identity of Little John, who had no taxable income. Little John assumed the identity of a tinker and went underground. And the king's deer in Sherwood Forest kept disappearing whenever the little band of outlaws decided it was time to feed the poor.

MISS MINSK
OUTDOOR LIFE
V. J. 85

Raskolnikov

(last seen in Dostoevsky's Crime and Punishment*)*

For the premeditated axe murder of two elderly women, Rodion Raskolnikov was sentenced to eight years in Siberia. Raskolnikov had tried to commit the "perfect crime." And nothing stood in the way of his freedom but his conscience. His guilty babbling to Police Inspector Porfiry Petrovich finally did him in.

But after a few months in Siberia, Raskolnikov had a change of heart. In a letter to his faithful girl friend, Sonya Marmeladov, he wrote he was hoping to get his freedom, or at least a weekend pass. A packet of Raskolnikov's letters to Sonya was recently discovered by the same source that gave you *The Hitler Diaries*.

"I am now rehabilitated," he announced. "I am also sane. Besides, I am a victim of the social system. Nobody should have so little upward mobility that he should be compelled to kill two old ladies as society forced me to do. On the basis of my roots in the community alone, I should be able to get parole soon. I am counting on you to help me. Your prisoner of love, (signed) Rodion."

There is no record that the Siberian parole board acted on any of his requests. Raskolnikov was born too soon.

Margot Macomber

(last seen in Ernest Hemingway's "The Short Happy Life of Francis Macomber")

"The Short Happy Life of Francis Macomber" ended with the death of the title character when his wife Margot accidentally—or so we may assume—shot him with a 6.5 Mannlicher while aiming at a charging bull buffalo. What happened to Margot after that has long been a matter of speculation, until the recent discovery (in an abandoned Abercrombie & Fitch warehouse) of notes for a book to be entitled "Buncombe in the Bush: Margot Macomber's Own Story, As Told to J. J. Pithhelmet." As the author cannot be found, we feel safe in transcribing his nearly illegible notes:

There was an inquest, of course. Mrs. Macomber was acquitted on all counts, supported by the testimony of Robert Wilson and two of his native gunbearers speaking in Swahili.

As for Wilson, the great white hunter put the whole affair down as a "rum go" and "ruddy rot" and he vowed to have nothing further to do with female clients ("blasted nuisances").

Having inherited her late husband's estate, Margot had no financial worries and nothing to do but to enjoy the dolce vita in Europe and America. But she could hardly be unaware of the whispers that followed in her wake—"Do you think she really tried to miss him?" being one of the more indelicate questions. "Doing a Macomber" became international code for Divorce, African Game-Hunt Style.

There were two, or possibly three, husbands more and a string of lovers whose names were known in gossip columns. As Margot slipped inexorably into middle-age, her beauty but slightly faded, a certain pinched look of discontent was evident in her photographs in *Vogue* and *Harper's Bazaar*.

Then came the stock market crash. Margot was wiped out, or as Walter Winchell put it, "Margot and her millions are *pfft*."

Bravely, she carried on. In her later years she operated a gift shop in Beverly Hills called "Safari So Good," devoted to exotic imports, objects from Africa mainly, gazelle-hoof ashtrays, gnu-bone fingerbowls, hartebeest haberdashery, crocodile-skin underwear, that sort of thing. When the store was replaced by a fat-off exercise disco, Margot had a brief fling as a movie-colony celebrity.

She remained cheerful and often predicted that one day she would be rich again.

"Sure as shooting," she would say.

Robert Aldrich

Pagliaccio—a.k.a. Canio

(last seen in Leoncavallo's Pagliacci*)*

Canio, whose stage name was Pagliaccio, served eighteen months in the Calabria Correctional Facility for the murder of his wife, Nedda, and her lover, Silvio. His sentence was light because his act was judged a "crime of passion." Pagliaccio emerged from prison a changed man. He left show business and devoted the rest of his life to social reform.

An old file of the *Montalto Daily Courier* reveals that he had founded a group to combat violence in operatic libretti.

"Too much stabbing," Pagliaccio complained. "In opera, the singers die like flies. Look! In *Cavalleria Rusticana*, Turiddu is stabbed by a jealous husband. In *Rigoletto*, Gilda is stabbed by an assassin and the body is given to her father in a sack. In *Il Trovatore*, Leonora is poisoned and Manrico is hanged. Tosca commits suicide by jumping from a high place. Cio Cio San stabs herself to death. And for what?

"The only sopranos who die natural deaths are Mimi and Violetta. Both terminal cases of TB. It's got to stop."

Asked what program he recommended, Pagliaccio answered in one word: "Handguns." He explained: "Arm the tenors. Let them carry pistols. The tenors are usually the good guys. Then those creeps and punks will think twice about offing the hero."

Before his death, in 1960, Pagliaccio wrote the bestseller, *100 Safest Operas*.

Robinson Crusoe

(last seen in Farther Adventures*, a sequel to Daniel Defoe's classic)*

After Robinson Crusoe returned and settled down in England, he spent a lot of time defending his reputation against insinuations in the yellow press. One especially scurrilous story claimed that Friday was so named because Crusoe kept four women named Monday, Tuesday, Wednesday, and Thursday. And a certain Charity Wiggins came out with a memoir entitled: *I Was a Love Slave.* She alleged that she had been a passenger on the shipwrecked craft on which Crusoe had sailed. "It was I who taught him how to sew," she wrote. And she explained that she had come aboard the rescue vessel concealed under a pile of goat skins for reasons of propriety. (Charity had a husband back home, who subsequently passed away.)

Crusoe vigorously fought these libelous stories in court.

To pay his lawyers' fees, Crusoe launched a company that sold marine insurance. Its motto was "Don't Leave Home Without It." As salesmen, Crusoe imported several natives of Juan Fernandez, the island on which he had been shipwrecked. "They know the territory," he explained.

Jo March

(last seen in Louisa May Alcott's Little Women*)*

Jo March married Professor Bhaer, and when Aunt March willed them her Connecticut home, Plumfield, the Bhaers went there to open a boys' school.

Jo enjoyed being a headmaster's wife, but her real ambition was to write. Every evening, after the boys were tucked into bed, Jo worked on a novel. The story of this book came to light recently in a journal that turned up when Plumfield was torn down to make way for a Burger King. Here are few random entries:

My ms. has now been at the publisher's for four years. Dare I write to enquire?

Rec'd letter of acceptance from publisher. Won't Marmee be thrilled! The bad news is that they want to call it "Little Women: The Untold Story." They offer no advance, but the royalty is generous, .001 percent.

There will be a publication party at Rector's next month! The publisher says that I will be billed for it. It's in my contract.

No ads in paper and I can't find the book anywhere in the stores.

Professor Bhaer has put the book on the Plumfield required reading list.

Rec'd the publisher's annual statement today. Eighteen copies of the book had been sold. Will inquire about the error, since at least twenty-seven copies were bought by our students at Plumfield as their English text, and twenty-eight as text for first-grade math, where they are taught in an innovative way to count words.

Having a meeting with Meg, Amy, and Marmee to decide what to do.

Little Red Riding-Hood

(last seen in the oeuvre of the Brothers Grimm)

After her close call, Little Red Riding-Hood was left with a distinct fear of wolves. An alchemist diagnosed it as acute Lupophobia, probably rooted in an Electra Complex.

This early therapist prescribed weekly sessions at three ducats per visit, to talk about Ms. Riding-Hood's early childhood, the root of her emotional problems. After a few sessions, she learned from the healer that there had really been no wolf at all. The wolf was an imaginary substitute for her father, whom she wanted to marry, and her grandmother stood for her mother, whom she wanted to do away with. The whole thing was a fantasy, said the physician, and understanding its symbolism would help her adjust to real life.

Little Red Riding-Hood was getting on well with her therapy. She graduated to "group," which lowered her hourly fee (and raised the alchemist's). There, she was rapping with a bunch of people, one of whom looked decidedly like a frog, though he had delusions of being a prince.

All was going well, when on one journey to the alchemist's office, she was eaten by a wolf.

RED

Dracula

(last seen in Bram Stoker's Dracula*)*

When an urban redevelopment program bulldozed Count Dracula's estate and burial site in Transylvania, it dislodged the stake from the vampire's heart. Dracula was again at large!

But Transylvania was now part of the Eastern bloc and Dracula found it difficult to circulate without an I.D. He finally found lodgings in a sleazy boarding house in Bucharest. The concierge, a police informer, fingered the count as an "aristocrat" and he fled one jump ahead of the Rumanian secret police.

With some gold coins that he had sewn into his cape, Dracula bought a fake passport and a flight to the USA. Landing at JFK in New York, Dracula directed the cab driver to take him to "the center of town." He was dropped at 42nd Street and Broadway, where he attracted no attention whatsoever.

But he had a hard time with the English he was hearing.

"What means 'dealing'?" he asked a passing stranger.

The man called him a "narc" and spat on Dracula's shoe. A shifty-looking bystander approached him. "What kind of fix you want, man?"

"Blood," gasped Dracula, as he felt an anxiety attack coming on for lack of nourishment.

"You better get yourself to a hospital, man," said the dealer, walking away.

Fortunately for Dracula, he checked into a teaching hospital, where more blood is taken from patients than there's need for. He spent his nights combing the lab for all the leftovers he could get. And days, he spent working as an extra in music-video productions.

Heathcliff

(last seen in Emily Brontë's Wuthering Heights*)*

Heathcliff's love, Catherine, had been seen on the moors off and on. But of Heathcliff himself, there were no reported sightings. So we went to the headquarters of psychic research, the Stanford Research Institute, which had certified the psychic power of Uri Geller.

To get in touch with Heathcliff, we would have to go to Wuthering Heights, the e.s.p. researchers told us. Ghosts don't travel well, and never answer the phone.

The séance was a great success. In a darkened room, Heathcliff's spirit told us that he was into an open marriage with his wife, Isabella. It allowed room for his lifelong love, Catherine. That was why, when they missed a tryst, you could hear a plaintive voice calling to him across the moors: "Heathcliff!"

Sometimes the voice would be harsher and more insistent—but that would be the voice of Isabella—and very often "Heathcliff!" would be followed by "Your dinner is getting cold!"

Captain John Yossarian

(last seen in Joseph Heller's Catch-22*)*

Finding Yossarian was not too difficult. We traced him through the Veterans Administration. He had never dropped his GI insurance, and the VA knew where to find him.

"After all that crazy stuff," Yossarian said, "I came back from Sweden, checked myself into a base hospital, and got a medical discharge. Otherwise I would have been jailed as a deserter. Now I'm trying to pay my debt to society. I've devoted my life to work that has redeeming social value. It hasn't been easy."

He spent one full year developing a system whereby he could restore vitality to fallen soufflés—until he discovered that the fallen soufflé was largely a myth.

He then turned to pedagogy and organized classes in the art of opening pill bottles with safety caps that made the pills inaccesible to children and everyone else. He did fairly well at this until he came across a new pill bottle that he himself could not open. He abandoned his classes because only a charlatan could continue to teach a subject he had not mastered.

At last he discovered his true métier. After making an extensive survey, he realized that certain qualities of Saran Wrap annoyed thousands of men and women. They liked the uses to which they could put Saran Wrap, but they were driven crazy by the wrap's tendency to stick to itself, particularly at the corners. Everyone knows how frustrating it is to tear off a perfect square of Saran Wrap, only to have one or more corners fold in upon themselves. Many people spend long and unrewarding hours trying to straighten out the product.

Yossarian became a Saran Wrap straightener. He mastered the art, and no matter how strongly the corners of Saran Wrap might self-adhere, he is always able to get that delicate little hold on the almost indistinguishable edge, and straighten it out. Yossarian makes house calls and he has endeared himself to many because of his willingness to respond to distress at any hour of the day or night. He is known and respected in his chosen profession and the years have brought him the plaudits and honors of his fellow man.

IRA WALLACH

Dorian Gray

(last seen in Oscar Wilde's The Picture of Dorian Gray*)*

From a recent catalogue of Christie's:

"#395. Portrait by Basil Hallward of Edwardian dandy. Mint condition, with traces of extensive restoration. One owner."

Bidding was spirited and the portrait went for 28,000 pounds to a dealer in fin-de-siècle kitsch, who was reputedly an agent for Boy George. He said his client planned to hang the portrait in his attic.

Captain Ahab

(last seen in Herman Melville's Moby Dick*)*

It was commonly believed that Captain Ahab died when his boat, the *Pequod*, was rammed and sunk by Moby Dick. But one day, a whaler out of New Bedford retrieved a floating bottle in which there was a note. The note read: "Help! I am a prisoner in a white whale. (signed) Ahab, Capt."

From this, the belief grew that Ahab had not been killed by the whale, but swallowed. This story gained credibility when, five years after the wreck of the *Pequod*, a gaunt and very pale American castaway was picked up off the coast of Patagonia. He claimed to be Ahab, and left an unpublished manuscript entitled: "Moby Dick: The Inside Story."

The manuscript found its way to the Widener Library at Harvard, from which it mysteriously vanished. An FBI investigation suggested that the manuscript had been stolen and destroyed by the literary mafia, which did not want to disturb the growing "Melville industry." (Academicians would have to consider the question, if Ahab was a Jonah, what does that make the whale?) But no firm evidence was found on which to press charges.

Almustafa

(last seen in Kahlil Gibran's The Prophet*)*

Almustafa the Prophet left the city of Orphalese promising to return. He did.

He looked for the quiet house overlooking the sea where he had once contemplated infinity—but it was now a luxury condo and the lobby attendant told him to move on. He sought Almitra, the seeress, with whom he had been in such close rapport. But she had been dispossessed when a high-rise had gentrified her studio and she left no forwarding address.

"Is there no haven in Orphalese where I can find shelter?" he cried aloud. Passersby gave him funny looks and one of them snarled, "Creep!"

For eleven days Mustafa wandered the streets, eating an occasional meal of singed souvlaki from a street vendor and sleeping in the bus terminal.

While he slept, a thief stole his shoes. On the twelfth day, Mustafa went down to the waterfront and willed his ship to come and bear him away to the isle of his birth. On the seventh hour of the fourteenth day it came. But it could not tie in to the rotting pier, so Mustafa had to swim out to board his ship. As he was hauled up over the side, dripping in effluence from the foul-smelling harbor, he was heard to say: "Ere I return, it will be a month of Sundays."

Merlin the Magician

(last seen in Thomas Malory's Morte d'Arthur*)*

Merlin was imprisoned under a rock by the ladies of the lake. The thinking was that he would stay there eternally.

But an earthquake dislodged the rock under which Merlin was imprisoned. He wandered out into an eight-lane highway and narrowly escaped being run over. A passing motorist gave him a ride into London. "Fancy dress ball?" he asked. Merlin nodded.

Merlin went into Harrod's to buy some clothes more suitable than the wizard's robe he was wearing. He was trying to convince a sales clerk to accept gold florins instead of a credit card when there was a terrifying explosion. Harrod's had been blown up by terrorists. Merlin staggered out with his robe in shreds. He was taken by ambulance to a hospital where he bled for an hour while an admitting clerk took down his medical history. When he gave his residence as "Camelot," he was taken to the psychiatric ward.

Merlin escaped in his nightshirt and a hospital bathrobe and wandered his way to Trafalgar Square, where he was astonished at the sight of baldheaded women. "Whatever happened to flaxen hair?" he muttered.

He tried to enter a restaurant in Mayfair and was thrown out because he wasn't wearing a tie.

A young man with a safety pin earring tried to sell him amphetamine. Remembering his magical powers, Merlin turned him into a toad. Then he hailed a cab by sorcery (the only way he could get one) and commanded the cabbie to take him back to his rock.

AMER A LOVES
RUDKUS
QUALITY MEATS
ALL NATURAL
100% PURE
PURE STEROIDS · PURE HORMONES
PURE CHEMICAL ADDITIVES & COLORS

Jurgis Rudkus

(last seen in Upton Sinclair's The Jungle*)*

Jurgis worked in the Chicago stockyards at a time when workers used to fall into the pickling vats and blood poisoning was an occupational hazard. Then he worked in a fertilizer plant, where the average life span before TB set in was two years. He was widowed tragically.

Jurgis eventually married Marija, his wife's cousin, and they had a son, Jurgis Rudkus, Jr., whom we interviewed. He was in the livestock business, which, he explained, was a family tradition. But he owned his own feed lot, and was about to retire in favor of his son, Jurgis Rudkus III.

We asked about the health hazards described in *The Jungle*, where his father had worked, and Jurgis laughed heartily.

"Animals are kept healthy nowadays," he explained. "They get penicillin with their feed. Fall into a pickling vat today, and you come out a healthy man."

We asked whether this doesn't breed new strains of disease.

"Consumerist propaganda!" he snorted. "Plus the livestock gets female hormones to help them fatten up."

We asked if this couldn't cause sex problems with the workers handling the feed.

Rudkus reddened. "Disinformation!" he shouted in a falsetto. He told us that the animals were restrained in pens, pretty much like chickens, in the interest of efficient management.

"Is this humane?" we asked. Rudkus got to his feet, his face a violent red, and we said a quick goodbye. His father had been a violent man, we recalled—and the son was a chip off the old butcher's block.

Ilsa and Victor Laszlo

(last seen leaving the movie Casablanca *in an airplane)*

Despite her love for Rick, Ilsa understood that her duty was to her husband Victor Laszlo, who was determined to win the Second World War. She and Victor spent the following year delivering messages to the Free French, the Yugoslav underground, and the Greek, Bulgarian, and Albanian resistance movements. By the time the war ended, Ilsa had forgotten Rick. She enjoyed carrying messages, because it helped her get away from Victor, who was a big bore.

At the end of the war, Victor brought Ilsa to New York City. Victor, dismayed by the turn of postwar world events, took a decided turn to the right in matters political. Ilsa, however, remained considerably left of center. This clash of philosophies inevitably led to divorce.

Ilsa joined the America Labor Party and twice ran for the New York City Council. She lost both times, and after each election, she made a stirring speech to prove that her loss was a victory. Then she turned her attention to consumer affairs and then to environmental issues, and she was credited with saving thirty-two whales single-handedly. During this period she married a dedicated environmentalist who was leading the struggle to put the house fly on the endangered species list. Today she is incredibly old but this does not deter her from delivering meals on wheels to others even older than herself.

As for Victor, he became a political analyst and made such a name for himself that he was invited to join the editorial staff of *Commentary* magazine. While on the staff, he tried desperately to occupy a position to the right of Norman Podhoretz, but there was no room. Having lost that fight, he resigned from the magazine and devoted his remaining days to being very bitter.

IRA WALLACH

Howard Roark

(last seen in Ayn Rand's The Fountainhead*)*

Howard Roark was arrested in midtown New York when he was found in the basement of the World Trade Center with a suitcase of dynamite, a detonator, and an alarm clock.

"Ugly! Ugly!" he is reported to have screamed: "I was willing to blow up perversions of my own work—right? I'm sure as hell willing to blow up other architectural mutants! Philip Johnson should design toilet seats! Le Corbusier—what a phony! All of these cookie-cutter ice-cube trays on end have got to go!"

Roark was taken to Bellevue Hospital, for psychiatric observation. He escaped. He left a note which was not revealed, but police have posted a special guard around Trump Tower.

Harry Haller

(last seen in Hermann Hesse's Steppenwolf*)*

Haller a.k.a. "Steppenwolf" stabbed his paramour Hermine in the chest. Whereupon his friend Pablo, the drug dealer and sax player, shrank Hermine to the size of a figurine and slipped her into his pocket.

Well, information has turned up that Harry bought the Hermine doll from Pablo for a fifth of schnapps and took it to a dwarf in the Black Forest.

This tiny craftsman, whose name was O. A. F. Schwartz, rebuilt the figure into a life-size inflatable doll. When Harry's friends Maria and Pablo saw the doll, they wanted one too. Harry went into the inflatable business with Schwartz until World War II, when they adapted their product to rubber dinghies that could be used as convertible inflatable dolls in a pinch.

An item in a Berlin newspaper noted that the Haller-Schwartz factory was destroyed by a fire started when one of the inspectors fell asleep with a cigarette while testing a dinghy-doll.

V.J.'85

Frankenstein's Monster

(last seen in Mary Shelley's Frankenstein*)*

After seeing Victor Frankenstein die on a boat in the Arctic Circle, the monster he had made disappeared into the frozen wastes.

"The reports of my death were greatly exaggerated by the movie," he later said.

He wasn't sighted for many years.

Then one day he turned up in Juneau, Alaska, where he was immediately recruited for the basketball team. Reluctantly the coach had to let him go. The creature was a great shot but a poor dribbler.

When last in the public eye, the monster was being touted as a candidate for public office. He had all the essentials for politics: high visibility and a knack for speaking in simple, understandable language. But that fell through when no talk show host (with the exception of Phil Donahue) would have him as a guest. There was also some talk among a group of New York citizens of hiring him to stalk the subways at night. But that came to nothing when a group of activists from Scarsdale, in for the day to paste daisy decals on a block of houses in the inner city, cried, "Vigilantism!"

The monster disappeared once more and has never again been seen. But giant footprints in the snow, formerly attributed to Big Foot are believed by some to belong to the missing monster, who wore size 18 mukluks.

Trilby O'Ferrall

(last seen in George Du Maurier's Trilby*)*

When Trilby was hypnotized by Svengali, she could sing in an operatic soprano that enthralled concert audiences. When Svengali died, Trilby regained her natural singing voice, which was a monotone croak.

In her obituary it was noted that she had formed a combo with a drummer and a guitarist and sung in the streets of Paris for coins from passersby. It was a living, but not much more. Rock was still fifty years away.

Trilby realized that what she needed was a new hypnotist. She found one on the variety hall circuit. But all he could do was make her quack like a duck.

Finally, Trilby teamed up with a ventriloquist she had met on the road. With his help, she sang in a deep baritone. It wasn't operatic stardom, but it was a show stopper.

Jane Eyre

(last seen in Charlotte Brontë's novel)

Jane Eyre married Edward Rochester after his house burned down with the first Mrs. Rochester in it.

Jane and Rochester had their first difference of opinion over where they would live. Rochester wanted to rebuild Thornwood. "If we ever reappear in fiction," he said, "I want to be in a Gothic novel."

Jane preferred to settle down in a flat.

"What?" Rochester responded. "And be in a flat novel? Never."

True to her Victorian self-image, Jane agreed.

Estimates for rebuilding Thornwood were high. The builder said the costs were increased by Rochester's insistence on frills, like echo chambers and locked rooms within rooms on the third floor.

"Locked rooms on the top floor and echo chambers are part of my lifestyle," Rochester insisted.

Neighbors gave the marriage six months.

When Rochester began seeing too much of his old flame, Blanche Ingram, Jane decided it was time to make her move. She collected her portable assets and took up residence in the home of her cousin, the Rev. St. John Rivers.

Eventually, Rivers and Jane went to India as missionaries, where they turned up in a series on Masterpiece Theater under different names.

Jonathan Livingston Seagull

(last seen in Richard Bach's book flying at empyrean heights into what may have been either a sunrise or a sunset, depending on whether you were standing on your feet or your head)

In the course of his last magnificent flight, Jonathan Livingston Seagull looked down and saw far below the outlines of a building housing a well-known Amagansett fishmarket. Jonathan cut back on the power and entered a descending spiral glide. He noticed on a small expanse of lawn in back of the fishmarket a most appealing collection of discarded fish heads, crown rack of gills, tails, post-fillet bones, and other finny tidbits strewn carelessly about as though they were of no value. Jonathan came to rest in the middle of the lawn. Reassured when the few men who saw him made no threatening gestures, he settled down and proceeded to stuff his gut until his belly distended and even his feathers grew fat.

When he could eat no more, he settled down for a snooze, but before he fell asleep he reflected sadly on his wasted youth, the years he had spent soaring with the wind currents, fighting the tempest, and scouring the Atlantic for signs of a square meal swimming beneath the briny. When he thought of how much blood, sweat, and tears he had invested in the simple process of gorging himself, he wept, for here, in the backyard of the Amagansett fish market, all the treasures of the sea were readily available without so much as a beat of the wing.

Jonathan Livingston Seagull has never left the backyard of the fish market. There he has grown old, not gracefully but contentedly. Instead of flying, he now waddles. His life has been celibate but, as he remarked to a passing crow, "When you have enough fish heads, who needs sex?"

Ira Wallach

Daisy Buchanan

(last seen in F. Scott Fitzgerald's The Great Gatsby*)*

After the hit-and-run accident in which Daisy Buchanan killed Myrtle Wilson, she went to the police and tried to confess. "I was at the wheel of Jay Gatsby's car when it hit Myrtle," she explained. "And just for the record, Jay was shot by Myrtle's husband, because my husband Tom told her husband that Jay had been sleeping with Myrtle. But it wasn't Jay. It was Tom who was playing around. Do you understand?"

"Certainly lady," said the desk sergeant. "Why don't you go home and sleep it off." Over the years, Daisy remained obsessed with her guilt, until she went to a nursing home in the 1960s. As it turned out, the nursing home was located in an old mansion converted by real estate developers from the old Gatsby place in West Egg. "It feels like home," Daisy told an interviewer.

Rip Van Winkle

(last seen in Washington Irving's The Legend of Sleepy Hollow*)*

Rip Van Winkle kept a journal in which he updated his adventures. It turned up in a flea market in Sullivan County, upstate New York. It is now in the P. J. Morgan Library (not to be confused with the Morgan Library in New York City, which doesn't include bed and breakfast).

The journal recounts how Van Winkle's life was made intolerable by tourists and curiosity seekers. So the next time he heard the rumble of a thunderstorm, he went roaming in the Catskills and ran into the same crew of dwarfs bowling ten pins. The result was another twenty-year nap.

He woke up during the Civil War, served as a Union scout, and went back into the Catskills for another siesta. This time Van Winkle slept longer than usual. When he awoke, he came down from the mountains and as he was walking into town he was hit by a station wagon.

The driver took him to the new community hospital, where they set his broken leg and took his medical history. A resident medic diagnosed Rip's ailment as "narcolepsy" and prescribed amphetamines to help him keep awake.

That's as far as the journal goes. But guests at Grossinger's in the Catskills claim to have seen a bearded man with bulging eyes in funny clothes.

He said he was looking for the bowling alley.

Faust

(last seen in Marlowe's Dr. Faustus, *Goethe's* Faust, *etc.)*

We interviewed Faust at his office in Faust International, a major producer of music videos. He was an open-faced man of about forty-five, with a ready smile. But when we lit a cigarette, he frowned.

"I don't mind the smoke," he said, "But I don't like the flame. Do you mind?"

We stubbed it out in an ashtray shaped like a cloven hoof. We expressed surprise at finding him so easily. He laughed. "I've never gone underground," he said, slapping his thigh. "Get it? Wherever I operate—in discos, or videos, or commodity futures—my name is always on the front door."

We mentioned that there were conflicting stories about him. Goethe said that he ascended to heaven and Marlowe put him in hell.

Faust laughed. "Lies. All lies. I sold my soul to the devil. Certainly. And I've been doing the devil's work ever since. You see, my first contract was for twenty-four years—with options. I've always been renewed. Lots of folks sold their souls to my employer. But I have the record for the longest continuous employment. The secret is—you got to pick your spots. And sometimes I get a call from headquarters." He pointed to a red telephone. "On the hot line."

"I've been in condo conversions, union leadership, big business, city politics, building inspecting, you name it."

What was his next move?

"I was thinking of oil—petroleum. But the field is too overcrowded. So I'm going to concentrate on politics."

He pointed to a poster which read VOTE FOR FAUST FOR SURROGATE. "Wills and estates. Probate. It will always be a hell of a business."

Tarzan

(last seen in Edgar R. Burroughs' Tarzan and the Foreign Legion*)*

Tarzan was not at home when we visited the Greystoke condo in Tarzana, California, where Lord and Lady Greystoke (Mr. and Mrs. Tarzan) have been spending their golden years. Lady Jane laughed at the suggestion that Tarzan had retired. "Heavens no," she said. "Tarzan is busier than ever." She explained that the Ape Man had been a psychotherapist since the end of World War II. "We had to find some occupation for which there were no formal requirements. Tarzan doesn't have a high school diploma, you know.

"But," she added proudly, "now he conducts seminars in the primal scream."

Alexander Portnoy

(last seen in Philip Roth's Portnoy's Complaint*)*

We found Alexander Portnoy at the Yeshiva College, where he is a research fellow. Asked whether this was not an incongruous discipline for someone with his lifestyle, Portnoy smiled patiently. "That mommser Roth," he said wearily. "Anything for a laugh. If I had spent my time the way he has it, I would have grown hair between my fingers. You can check this out with Dr. Spielvogel.

"I've always been deeply interested in Judaic studies. When I was New York's assistant commissioner of human opportunity, I worked for a Ph.D. in Jewish history. Passed my orals." He reddened slightly and continued. "And for the record—my mother was a saint!"

Larry

(last seen in Somerset Maugham's The Razor's Edge*)*

When Larry returned from his voyage of self-discovery and spiritual renewal, there were presumably only two people who clearly understood what it was that he had found: Somerset Maugham and Larry himself.

That was in the year 1938. Thirty years later, Larry himself began wondering exactly what it was that he had learned. By that time, he was living in the suburbs with a wife and kids in a house with a two-car garage.

One morning, after rising, Larry asked his wife to pack him a lunch because he was going out and might not return until late. When she asked where he was going, he replied, "To search for the truth I once knew, and now forgot."

He returned late that night, footsore and bone-weary.

"Did you find truth?" asked his wife.

"Not today," he said, "but I'm going to try again tomorrow."

He tried every day for three months. By that time his wife was beginning to have second thoughts about the marriage and she longed for the day when the children would be big enough to move out of the house.

Then Larry took down his two largest suitcases and began to pack for a long trip. "I'm going back to the Himalayas," he explained, "to see an old holy man who lives on top of a very high mountain."

"You'll catch your death," his wife muttered to herself, scarcely aware that this was wishful thinking.

Larry reached the Himalayas, where it took him four painful days to climb the cruel mountain atop which lived the aged wise man. Larry struggled against a bitter wind and a driving snow to reach the cave where the old man lived. Inside the cave, he found the wizened seer huddled against a rock wall, trying to wrap his threadbare shawl more closely around his fleshless body.

"Old man," said Larry, "tell me, what is truth?"

"It's very cold," said the old man.

"What was that?"

"You wanted to know the truth, didn't you?"

"Yes," said Larry.

"Well, the truth is that it's very cold."

Larry never left the cave. How could he go back, face his wife, and tell her what the truth was? If he did, she might demand a fuller explanation.

Abandoned, his wife and her four children sank into abject poverty, where they remain until this day.

IRA WALLACH

Mr. Mellors

(last seen in D.H. Lawrence's Lady Chatterley's Lover*)*

Mr. Mellors, the gamekeeper, married Constance Chatterley, but it didn't work out. Lady Chatterley felt that she could have an orgasm only on an army blanket, while Mellors now insisted on "a proper bed." Their sex life deteriorated to a point where Mellors claimed that Connie was "faking it," and he had to escalate his sex fantasies from the national average of seven daily. The Mellorses had an amicable divorce and Constance married Fairfield Sturgeon, a baronet with a thousand acres of uncultivated land in Northumberland. On his wife's recommendation, Lord Sturgeon hired Mellors as gamekeeper.

Lady Brett Ashley

(last seen in Hemingway's The Sun Also Rises*)*

Mrs. Ashley was interviewed in the London offices of Lady Brett Cosmetics, manufacturers of "Night In Pamplona" and other worldwide beauty-care preparations. She has been long divorced from Michael Campbell, by whom she had one son.

Asked why she had never remarried, she explained: "I suppose I simply got fed up with being a sex object. Bob, Mike, Pedro, and poor Jake—all they wanted was one thing. I felt that I had to grow. And when I was into a more mature lifestyle, I came to realize there was more in life than making out."

"What about the Lost Generation?" she was asked.

"Poppycock," laughed Lady Brett. "That was just a piece of wonderful hype dreamed up by dear Gertrude. Living high on the hog in Paris is not what I call 'lost.' What's truly lost is *this* generation. Take my grandson Mike, Jr." Her blue eyes grew misty. "Three years with a rock group. Two years in an ashram. Now he's recovering from an underdose of macrobiotics." She dabbed her eyes with a Lady Brett tissue. "And he never calls."

PURITANS
DO IT
WITH
GUILT

Hester Prynne

(last seen in Nathaniel Hawthorne's The Scarlet Letter *slipping into an article of clothing that bore a scarlet "A" monogram)*

When Hester Prynne first began wearing the garment that we now know as a T-shirt, its chic embroidered "A" caused her some embarrassment. Clearly, the "A" did not stand for Hester Prynne. When people asked her the meaning of the monogram, she said it stood for AMOUR, or AZYGOSPORE, or ASSOCIATIVE ALGEBRA. Then, when she decided to exercise her mind as well as her body, she studied ancient Greek and claimed that the letter "A" stood for AESCHYLUS, thus raising her standing in the New England academic community.

As the years passed, however, people began to admire Hester's exotic garment and rushed to buy T-shirts of their own emblazoned with such legends as ABSOLUTE POWER CORRUPTS ABSOLUTELY.

After her Greek period, Hester struck up a close friendship with Charity Partridge, with whom she would tipple of a weekend. It was to Charity that a slightly wine-drenched Hester confided that the "A" really stood for ADULTRESS. Charity was filled with envy. "Can I get one, too?" she asked.

"Certainly," said Hester, "but you have to earn it first. Remember: there are no free lunches."

Charity earned her "A" and from this small beginning she and Hester launched a thriving cottage industry manufacturing Prynne's A-T-Shirts. Then, in an effort to diversify, Prynne introduced a new line of M-T-Shirts, the "M" standing for MONOGOMY. The project was a failure.

IRA WALLACH

Igor

(last seen in the Hollywood version of Mary Shelley's Frankenstein*)*

Igor, you may recall, was constantly at the good doctor's beck and call, hustling up a human organ here, a corpse there.

But all the time there seethed within his breast the desire to make something monstrous of his own. Yes, Igor was jealous of his boss!

Well, after things went wrong, after the monster terrorized the land, arousing angry peasants who closed in on Frankenstein to wreck his laboratory and end his fabulous career, Igor was out of a job and left to wander the world on his own. As you may imagine, he found conditions difficult, especially when word of his identity got around.

"Hire Igor, that nogoodnick! Better we should hire the devil himself!" That just about sums up the prevailing attitude. And it's perfectly understandable. After all, Igor had assisted Dr. Frankenstein with science's first creation of a living being that went amok. It would be a miracle if some of the blame had not rubbed off on poor Igor, however innocent he might have been.

So for many months Igor was forced to beg for his bread or to work as a common laborer. Even that was difficult. What could he put after, "Who was your last employer?"

But one day his luck seemed about to change. A branch of General Electric hired him as junior engineer. (He did know a lot about turning on the juice.) One promotion led to another. Then Igor was brought to the United States by the same head hunters who recruited the German rocket scientists. He is now in the inner circle of advisers on nuclear weaponry. At last—Igor has a monster of his own.

Robert Aldrich

WE WAITED FOR YOU BUT YOU NEVER SHOWED UP.
Vladimir
Estragon
I STOPPED BY - MUST'VE MISSED YOU RIGHT AFTER YOU LEFT.
G.

Godot

(last heard of in Samuel Beckett's Waiting for Godot*)*

The two tramps Vladimir and Estragon waited endlessly for Godot. They considered hanging themselves, but they decided to wait until they saw what Godot had to say. Godot didn't show up. In the meantime, Vladimir and Estragon forgot what question they wanted to ask him.

Vladimir and Estragon tried to hang themselves, but they bungled the job when the tree branch they were using failed to support them both.

As it does for many near-suicides, being close to death gave Vladimir and Estragon a new lease on life. They became itinerant vendors.

When last seen they were pushing a souvlaki cart in New York City. The two tramps hadn't cleaned up their act much, but in New York nobody seems to mind unwashed derelicts as food handlers. Otherwise all the pretzel vendors, hot dog carts, and knish merchants would be out of business.

We asked the two ex-tramps if they still were expecting a visit from Godot.

"You wanna buy a souvlaki?" Vladimir asked. "Man, if you don't," said Estragon, "you're standing in our space."

Major Barbara

(last seen in Shaw's Major Barbara*)*

An old issue of the English tabloid *Tatler* tells what happened to Barbara Undershaft, a onetime major in the Salvation Army. She was interviewed in Barbara's Boutique, a trendy specialty shop in Carnaby Street.

"Daddy was a munitions maker, you know," said Ms. Undershaft. "A merchant of death, they used to call him. But he shook my faith. He convinced me that salvation lay not in religious conversion but in economic security provided by industry. Hah!" She paused to light a thin black cigar and went on. "Then World I came along and Daddy's munitions killed hundreds of thousands. Then came the Depression, and the factories closed. Daddy's employees joined the jobless millions."

And then? "And then I went to the Salvation Army and tried to get my old job back as a major. But they made me start at the bottom, as a private. Would you believe? I was given a spot in the pick-up department. Picking up old furniture, and odds and ends to be fixed up and sold to the needy."

She took a reflective puff of her cigar. "One day I passed an antique shop. The stuff we were practically giving away, they were selling for prices that were astronomical, my dear. I bought out most of the army's stock and started the first Barbara's Boutique."

The first? "Oh yes. This is now a franchise. There are boutiques in Birmingham, Leeds, and Liverpool. With the craze for camp, we're making it very big. I guess that Daddy was right in his way, about the need for making money. And so was the army. You might say I have the best of both worlds."

Yentl

(last seen in the movie Yentl, *produced and directed by Barbra Streisand. Starring Barbra Streisand. Coauthored by Barbra Streisand.)*

Yentl bought steerage passage to the United States and once aboard ship, resumed her female identity. (She remembered that on shipboard women and children were first.) When they docked in New York, she went back to being Yentl, completely knocking out a shipboard romance.

At first, Yentl had a hard time of it—being constantly pursued by men. So Yentl went back once again to being a woman. But in 1905, Orthodox Jewish congregations still did not engage female rabbis, or cantors. Even choirs were unheard of in synagogues. So she began to sing as a performer. At Bar Mitzvahs, club dates, and at an occasional concert in the Bronx.

She was sometimes heckled by audiences who had overdosed on the sacramental wine, but her quick wit got big laughs at the hecklers' expense.

An agent for the Keith Albee Vaudeville circuit happened to be present at a circumcision party at which she was singing, and he was so impressed with her voice and her wit that he convinced her to try the stage. She was an instant hit, working for many years in vaudeville under the name of Fanny Brice.

Alice

(last seen in Lewis Carroll's Through the Looking Glass*)*

Alice grew to maturity just in time for the birth of modern psychotherapy. Among the apocrypha of the Freud Archive is an exchange of letters between Alice and Dr. Sigmund Freud. He had read *Alice in Wonderland*.

"These fantasies of shrinking small and growing tall dangerous symptoms are," Freud wrote. (He could never get his English syntax straight.) "Also, squeezing down a rabbit's hole, finding babies that turn into pigs, plus der angst of decapitation . . . Das ist extremely serious." Freud recommended that Alice have part of her nose amputated by his friend the eye, ear, nose, and throat man, Dr. Fliess.

Before he discovered the couch, Freud believed that nasal surgery would increase mental health.

Alice declined and took a long sea voyage instead. The salt air smelled good, and she was eternally glad that she had hung on to her nose.

Sherlock Holmes

(last seen in A. Conan Doyle's The Return of Sherlock Holmes*)*

It looked like the end when Sherlock Holmes was pushed over the Reichenbach Falls by the evil Professor Moriarty. But he reappeared in a couple of adventures, only to disappear once again; this time without a trace.

What actually happened is recorded in one of Watson's diaries, which was partly destroyed by fire. Watson writes that on his advice, Holmes went to a detox sanitarium in Baden Baden, to cure himself of his cocaine habit.

Once Holmes had kicked the habit, he rediscovered his sex drive and lost interest in crime. Up to then, Holmes' only date had been with Irene Adler, the paramour of the King of Bohemia, who stood him up. But now Holmes was seen nightly in all the Mayfair hot spots.

Watson tried to get his old friend to marry and settle down, but Holmes wouldn't hear of it. "If I'm not near the girl I love," he would sing in his mellow baritone, "I love the girl I'm near." Then he would pick up his violin and play a few bars of the latest music hall hit.

This went on until Irene and her husband, a lawyer named Godfrey Norton, turned up again in London. Holmes began dating Irene whenever Godfrey was in court, but one day the lawyer came home early to surprise his wife and Holmes.

The Norton divorce was a messy cause célèbre. When it was concluded, Holmes and Irene were married and lived very happily at 221B Baker Street. As Watson's diary breaks off, Irene is enciente. If it is a boy, they plan for him to be a detective, and if a girl, an adventuress.

Aïda and Rhadames

(last seen in Verdi's opera Aïda *holding hands and breathing heavily in the Egyptian tomb in which they had been imprisoned)*

The pyramid-shaped crypt in which the lovers were entombed had a mysterious magnetic field which is just beginning to be understood. Without going into psychic technicalities: Aïda and Rhadames went into a trance from which they awoke in 1923. The first thing Rhadames noticed was a fissure in the wall of the tomb. He began hacking away at the wall with a random artifact and his efforts were quite successful, aided as he was by Aïda's high notes, which shattered some of the tougher stones. Three days and six arias later, they were free.

Once out, however, they had only their love to sustain them. Army service was now out of the question for Rhadames, and as for Aïda, she had only those skills which can be exercised in bed. So there they were, the wretched lovers, devoid of food, work, or even a roof over their heads. Again they burst into song to while away the time before death. Then Rhadames stopped Aïda's mouth just as she was about to squeeze out a high C.

"We got out of the tomb, little lollipop," he said, "so we can get back in."

Only when he had led her into the tomb once more did he explain. "This tomb," said Rhadames, "is full of artifacts. American tourists will pay a fortune for them."

They carried out as many artifacts as they could manage and sold them to American tourists at outrageous prices. Whenever they ran out of stock, they went back to the tomb for another load. In two years they made enough money to buy a villa in Alexandria.

The time came, however, when they stripped the tomb of its very last artifact. Aïda became morose, moody, and lethargic. Even Rhadames' protestations of eternal love failed to rouse her from her funk. Then Rhadames had another brainstorm. "Ooogums!" he cried (in Arabic), "the streets of Egypt are filled with artifacts!" And so they both collected artifacts from gutters, hallways, and garbage dumps. These sold just as well as the genuine articles from the tomb. Their fastest-moving item was a scarab pendant whose stone was a lump of petrified camel dung. The Americans highly value this scarab pendant.

By now, the lovers were solidly ensconced in Alexandria, where they lived to a fruitful old age, admired and respected by the community. When they died, they were buried in the same tomb from which they had escaped. Grieving friends and relatives filled the tomb with artifacts.

IRA WALLACH

Dr. Jekyll

(last seen in Robert Louis Stevenson's Dr. Jekyll and Mr. Hyde*)*

Mr. Hyde was found dead in the laboratory of Dr. Jekyll. A letter left in the possession of Jekyll's lawyer, Utterson, claimed that Jekyll and Hyde were the same person. But Utterson didn't buy it. Jekyll's will left his estate to Edward Hyde. Had the doctor changed his mind and killed Hyde? To Utterson's legal mind, this was a motive for mischief.

Records of the Old Bailey (destroyed in the Blitz) show that Utterson had charged Dr. Henry Jekyll in absentia with malpractice. By denying Hyde the drugs needed to sustain him, Dr. Jekyll had "pulled the plug" on Mr. Hyde.

Since there were no heirs of either Dr. Jekyll or Mr. Hyde, Utterson, as executor of the estate, put all of Dr. Jekyll's money into the Edward Hyde Foundation, with himself as the executor.

Maggie Shand

(last seen in J.M. Barrie's What Every Woman Knows*)*

For years Maggie Shand had been "typing" the speeches of her husband John, a member of Parliament, putting in the humor that Shand himself lacked. These bright spots became famous as "Shandisms." What Every Woman Knows is that behind every succesful man is a clever woman.

Maggie had been happy in her backstage role for some years, until she ran into Mrs. Emmaline Pankhurst, founder of the Women's Social and Political Union. Maggie joined this militant suffragist movement and was soon making speeches on her own. But they were duds. At feminist gatherings, the audiences sat on their hands. Maggie was crushed. Why could she write great speeches for John and not for herself?

Then John asked to see her latest speech. With a blue pencil, he took out some of the stuff here and there.

"Trust me," he said. "I've adapted this speech to suit your audience." When Maggie delivered this latest speech, she received a standing ovation.

John explained what he had done. "I just took out the humor," he said.

$1,000,000.00

Tom Joad

(last seen in John Steinbeck's The Grapes of Wrath*)*

After Tom Joad knocked down a deputy sheriff with an axe handle in a fight at a migrant labor camp, he had to flee the territory.

He eked out a bare living for many years. Until one day, when he was buying two gallons of non-premium gas at a dusty filling station somewhere in Oklahoma, a well-dressed stranger, stepped out of a Cadillac and walked up to him excitedly. The statute of limitations had long since run out, so Tom wasn't especially worried.

"How much do you want for your jalopy?" the stranger asked.

"It's not for sale," Tom answered. It wasn't worth much, but how else could he get around?

"I'll give you five for it," the dude said. Tom spun on his heel and climbed into his old Model "A" Ford. He may have looked hard up, but this dude had some nerve offering him five bucks.

He turned on the ignition. The engine made a hideous noise.

"How about ten?" yelled the man.

"What do you mean, ten?" Tom said angrily.

"I mean $10,000 cash on the barrelhead," the dude said.

With this transaction to inspire him, Tom made a sentimental journey to look up all his old friends from the sharecropping days. He bought out their entire assortment of flivvers. They thought he was crazy to offer them a hundred bucks apiece.

Then Joad branched out into other areas of junk. His collection of jelly glasses was recently auctioned at a black tie event at Christie's.

"One man's junk is another person's collectible," Tom explained. "I don't understand it, but I'm not fighting it."

Gregers Werle

(last seen in Henrik Ibsen's The Wild Duck*)*

Gregers Werle had a lifelong compulsion to tell the truth and to expose lies. When Hedvig shot herself because Werle had exposed her as his father's illegitimate daughter, he went into seclusion.

An old interview printed in the *Bergen* (Norway) *Tribune* revealed the subsequent career of Gregers Werle. It was one of a series of stories about the beginnings of successful entrepreneurs.

Interviewed in the offices of Werle Communications, Werle confessed that the death of Hedvig had opened his eyes. "I found," he said, "that telling the truth was pernicious. So what could I do with the rest of my life? I decided to devote it to telling lies. But how?

"I thought of public relations, advertising, politics—but these fields were too overcrowded. I briefly thought of going into storm window promotions, and even considered selling health insurance to people over eighty-nine. But then it came to me: I was going to start a news magazine: *Werle's World*." He paused reflectively. "Nobody has suffered from seeing the truth in *Werle's World*."

Nora

(last seen in Ibsen's A Doll's House*)*

After Nora slammed the door on her husband, Torwald, she went into the loan-sharking business with Krogstad, the ex-employee of her husband's who had tried to blackmail him. The sexist nature of Norwegian society made it necessary for Krogstad to act as a front man, although Nora was clearly the brains behind the firm.

Krogstad asked Nora to marry him, but she preferred the single lifestyle. Nora made a cause out of eliminating sexism from the language, and when she was able to buy a steam yacht (named *Doll*), she impressed the importance of this on the captain. Nora drowned when the *Doll* struck a reef and sank. Newspaper accounts say that there might have been more survivors had it not been for the confusion that ensued when the captain yelled to the crew, "Person the lifeboats!"

Tristan and Isolde

(last seen in Gottfried von Strassburg's Tristan und Isolde. *Also used by R. Wagner as an opera libretto)*

Tristan was in love with Isolde, who was betrothed to his uncle, King Mark of Cornwall. To keep himself out of mischief, Tristan went into voluntary exile and devoted himself to acts of chivalry. At this point the story breaks off. But an old parchment records the rest of the story:

Tristan threw himself into killing dragons until dragons were declared an endangered species. He then became honorary chairman of the Save the Dragons Foundation and returned to Cornwall on a promotional campaign. At a mead and venison fund-raiser, King Mark was so impressed that he allowed Isolde to join Tristan on the tour.

They were never again heard from. Neither was the money raised on tour. Plus, it is now almost impossible to find a dragon anywhere.

"K"

(last seen in Franz Kafka's The Castle*)*

Kafka's "K" never did reach Castle West-west, where he was supposed to have a job as a surveyor. He remained marooned in a tavern in the town, where he became involved with three women named Frieda, Olga, and Amalia, and a sinister man named Jeremiah.

With the aid of a Central European road atlas, we located Castle West-west on the map and found it after some misdirection by unfriendly natives.

A huge neon sign proclaimed it to be Hilton West-west.

The reception desk was manned by a gray-faced clerk in a black blazer. A nameplate over his breast pocket read: "Jeremiah." We tried to book a room and pushed a handful of Czech currency across the desk. Jeremiah held up his hand. "No cash!" he said. "Only credit cards." When we told him we had no credit card, he shook his head vehemently. "We need credit cards for identity purposes," he said. "We can't register every Hans, Fritz, and 'K' who wants a room. You get my point? There was a fellow in the village some years ago who tried to reserve a room without proper documents. No way. He wrote a book about it."

Getting back to Prague from Hilton West-west took hours.

Frodo Baggins

(last seen in Tolkien's The Lord of the Rings*)*

As we know, Frodo took the bewitched Ring back to Mt. Doom, where it caused the mountain to erupt, obliterating the land of Mordor and quite a few of the hobbits' traditional enemies.

Then Frodo retired to the land of the elves, where we were able to reach him by phone. We taped the conversation:

Q: Frodo?

A: Frodo here.

Q: How are you?

A: Lousy. My old stab wounds ache every time it rains. Plus I've got a touch of hypertension. But Gandalf the wizard has whipped up a batch of herbal remedies that keep my pressure down. Not to worry.

Q: Then everything is okay?

A: Not really. There's nothing doing here in the Land of the Elves. What I miss most is the evil back in the Shire. I miss the orcs, those malicious demi-devils . . . I miss Shelob, the female spider monster, and Gollum, the traitor hobbit, the little creep. And Wormtongue the spy . . . Where are they now? Gone, and here I am. In the elves' Sun City. Bah. Humbug.

Q: Do you have a message for your fans?

A: Yes. Never retire!

(At this point we were disconnected. We tried to re-establish the connection. But the operator was a temp who insisted there was no area code for the Land of the Elves.)

Christopher Robin

(last seen playing with Winnie the Pooh in Winnie the Pooh *by A.A. Milne)*

In late adolescence Christopher Robin, soon to become a controversial figure in medical research, developed a passionate interest in animal dismemberment. After graduating from medical school with high honors, he did postgraduate work in Excoriation Biology.

Almost single-handedly, and against the protests of millions of misguided sentimentalists, Christopher Robin fought for an international program of koala bear dissection, work which resulted in significant advances in dandruff control and in alleviating the heartbreak of psoriasis.

In one amazingly bold coup, Christopher Robin stole unobserved into the People's Republic of China and dissected four pandas before making his way back to the Free World via Tibet. He then made his way to upstate New York, where he shot a bald eagle because, as he said, "I wanted to do my bit for avian population control." Forced by popular opinion to flee the region, he made his way to the Amazonian jungle where he met Rima, the Bird Girl, who bore him an illiterate son. He and Rima took turns sitting on the child, who soon became well-known for his densely matted hair.

Neither Rima nor the boy can communicate in any language, but they and Christopher find fulfillment in whistling at one another.

IRA WALLACH

PUCCINI
VERDI
PUCCINI
PUCCINI
VERDI
PUCCINI
BIZET
PUCCINI
MOZART
PUCCINI
La Bohème
PUCCINI
V.J. '85

The Flying Dutchman

(last seen in Wagner's Der Fliegende Hollander*)*

The Flying Dutchman was sighted from time to time by mariners. But in 1984, a satellite photo showed a spectral square rigger being boarded by a Soviet patrol boat in the Bering Straits.

Since then, there have been no further sightings.

Inquiries from the Dutch government have not been answered by the USSR. A Foreign Office spokesman explained that Captain Vanderdecken had been shooting dice with the devil for his soul, and that the outlook was not hopeful.

Soames Forsyte

(last seen in John Galsworthy's To Let, *the third volume of* The Forsyte Saga*)*

A search through the apocrypha in the British Museum turned up an interview with the elderly Soames Forsyte in the sales office of his development, Robin Hill estates.

"I've turned the house that I built for my rotten wife into a real estate project," he said.

The interviewer remarked that Soames looked spry and cheerful. "I am now," he said. "But for a long while I was in a dreadful funk. Look. My wife Irene fell in love with my architect and finally married my cousin Jolyon by whom she had a son, who fell in love with his stepsister Fleur, my daughter by my second wife, Annette. As if this weren't enough, my nephew Val married his cousin Holly. The Forsytes were beginning to look like the Jukes family." He took a sip of sherry.

And now? "Now I've thrown myself completely into my work. It's all that I can really depend on. I've invested every penny I've got in this housing scheme that I've made out of the family estate and it's going very well—1929 should be the best year yet."

A small item in a local paper in 1931 announced that Soames was now living with Val and Holly.

Hugh Conway

(last seen in James Hilton's Lost Horizon*)*

Conway, a British consul, left Shangri La, a Tibetan lamasery, where he was told he could have lived forever. But at the end of the book, he is trying to find his way back.

Conway did return to Shangri La. As promised, he was made High Lama. He presided wisely and happily. As did everyone else in Shangri La, he remained the same age as when he had arrived. Then came the boom in Buddhism in the 1960s. Conway began to be deluged with offers for his autobiography. Hardly a day went by without a call from some publisher or other, even though Shangri La's phone was unlisted.

Finally Conway signed a contract with an American publisher for his memoirs and spent a dozen years in writing them. The publisher thought Conway's manuscript lacked punch, and that it needed the author to make a publicity tour. Conway refused. Publication was delayed. At last, Conway consented to make an appearance on the last five minutes of the Johnny Carson Show, reserved for authors. He left Shangri La and, while en route, he died of old age. Publication of the book has been postponed until it can tie in with the movie, *Lost Horizon II*.

Martin Arrowsmith

(last seen in Sinclair Lewis's Arrowsmith*)*

We couldn't find Dr. Martin Arrowsmith listed in the American Physicians' Directory, so we took a chance at finding him in rural Vermont, where he had gone with his friend Terry Wickett to work on a cure for pneumonia.

"Arrowsmith?" the filling station attendent said. "Sure. There's a young guy who has some kind of a lab two and half miles down the highway." Young? Hmmm. The lab turned out to be a Bauhaus-type structure that looked like a mini-Guggenheim Museum.

"We're looking for Dr. Arrowsmith," we said to the young man in the lab coat who answered the door. "That's me," he said. "Come on in."

When we explained our mission, he took us into a small solarium, handed us a glass of carrot juice, and sipped one himself.

"I was wiped out by penicillin," he said. "Terry and I were into effective molds, when Fleming came out with his thing. So I just dropped out of medicine. It was a case of too much. Private practice was a rat race. Research could kill you, body or soul. Leora died in that epidemic in the West Indies. My big discovery went up in smoke. I was drunk for about a year. Then I was sent a trial subscription to *Prevention* magazine. It changed my life. No more artificial chemicals. I began to pursue Nature's Way!"

"In what direction?" we asked.

"Anti-oxydants," he said. "Old age retardants. How do I look?"

"Great," we said.

"You betcha," he said. "I'm my own guinea pig. But there are a few bugs in it. I took a bit of an overdose of my herbal formula, and I'm maybe a few years too young. But as soon as I fine-tune this thing, I'm going on Donahue. Meanwhile," he handed us a bound set of page proofs, "here's an advance copy of my book, *Live Longer! Look Younger!*"

"Take only as directed," he added.

HOWLERS

Buck

(last seen in Jack London's The Call of the Wild*)*

After Buck's master, Thornton, was killed by Indians, Buck returned to the forest and ran wild.

It was a reminder that Man was not to be trusted.

Then, he was adopted by a tenderfoot on a hunting vacation, and taken back East where he was used as a guard dog.

One night, a burglar broke into his master's house. Buck knocked the burglar down, and held the burglar's leg between his huge teeth until the police came.

Buck and his master were successfully indicted for using "excessive force."

The newspapers called Buck a "killer dog" and pointed out that the burglar had had an unhappy childhood. Before appealing the court decision, Buck's master called many newspapers to tell them the story of Buck's unhappy life—but they said that a dog's life is not news if it is led by a dog; only if it is led by a man.

When the dogcatcher arrived to take him away, Buck leapt through a window and headed north, never stopping until he was back in the Yukon. He spent the rest of his days with a pack of wolves who had a hereditary tradition of territorial rights—and whose behavior was governed by the law of the wild: If digestible, intruders were eaten.

Eliza Doolittle

(last seen in Bernard Shaw's Pygmalion*)*

Some hard losers insist on believing that Eliza returned to Professor Higgins. But that was just a screenwriter's gift to sentimentalists.

The fact is that Shaw wrote a special bulletin to assure one and all that after Eliza's crash course in elocution, she married Freddy Eynsford Hill and fulfilled her lifelong ambition. She opened a flower shop.

At the close of opening day, Eliza was so exhilarated that she brought a bouquet of roses to the man responsible for transforming her from a street vendor into a yuppie.

"Here, Professor Higgins," she said, "have a free gift."

Higgins' reaction was frightening. He turned white, then a violent red. "Free gift! You little numbskull!" he shrieked. "I spent three precious months of my life on your education, and your diction is no better than that of an . . . an advertising copywriter!" Eliza fled.

She had no idea why that nearly threw Higgins into an apopleptic fit, but thereafter, whenever she brought him some little item from the shop (a posy for his desk, or a boutonniere), she enclosed a bill.

Once he admired particularly an unusual bouquet of wild flowers she had brought. "It's *very* unique," Eliza announced—and fled, never to return, when Higgins' eyes began to cross.

Doctor Zhivago

(last seen in the novel by Boris Pasternak)

Dr. Zhivago did not die of a heart attack as is commonly believed. He did have an attack—of amnesia—and wandered away from his home. A neighbor's death certificate was incorrectly completed with Zhivago's name.

Zhivago could not remember his profession, so he was allowed to emigrate as an unskilled laborer. In New York City he began driving a taxi for one of the large fleets. He did not know the city very well, but neither did most of the other drivers.

One day, a passenger began giving birth to a baby while Zhivago's cab was on the Cross-Bronx Expressway. He immediately pulled into a service area and assisted in the birth of a fine 7½-pound girl. Zhivago called the paramedics on his car radio and an ambulance arrived to take mother and child away. "Gee, you were great," the woman said, as she was being lifted into the ambulance. "You should've been a doctor."

Doctor? This jogged Yuri Zhivago's dormant memory. Then, one day, a fare complained of a low-grade fever. "Take two aspirins and call me in the morning," Zhivago said absently. Suddenly he realized the significance of his advice. He *was* a doctor!

Immediately, Zhivago applied for his medical-school records and began studying for his New York license. Dr. Zhivago passed his exams and became a resident in internal medicine at one of the big metropolitan hospitals. It left him no time to write poetry, but that would come later. Once in private practice—he would be very hard to reach.

MOLL
FLANDERS

Fanny Hill

(last seen reunited with Charles, her first love, with whom she is determined to lead a life of exemplary virtue—in John Cleland's Memoirs of a Woman of Pleasure*)*

As Fanny Hill ruminated on her past, after leading the life of a bawd in eighteenth-century London, she could not "help pitying, even in point of taste, those who, immers'd in gross sensuality, are insensible to the so delicate charms of VIRTUE, than which even PLEASURE has not a greater friend, nor than VICE a greater enemy."

With Charles now sharing her life and her bed, Fanny determined to make amends for her past conduct, and it was she who founded the charter chapter of Virgins Anonymous in London. Membership was restricted to females because, as Fanny Hill rightly concluded, it would be counterproductive to bring men into an organization of women who needed outside help and encouragement in their efforts to maintain their VIRTUE. A message from any woman about to succumb to the allure of sexual VICE would bring a member of Virgins Anonymous to her side to give her the strength to resist. Within a few years, chapters of Virgins Anonymous functioned in all the major English, Scottish, and Welsh cities, and members, seated with their legs crossed, met regularly to discuss the forms of TEMPTATION and the means whereby to preserve INNOCENCE.

Fanny herself became increasingly virtuous, and although she did not deny herself to her beloved Charles, he found that with the passing years lovemaking became increasingly difficult, finally reaching such a degree of discomfort that he no longer visited her bed. Yet because he, too, was a devotee of VIRTUE, his love for her did not diminish.

Tragically, a minor outbreak of the PLAGUE claimed the life of Fanny Hill in her forty-second year. Charles grieved mightily, yet, perplexed by the physical changes in her that discouraged lovemaking, he permitted doctors to perform an autopsy. That autopsy revealed a miracle that is now part of medical history. Fanny Hill, in her fierce determination to eradicate her past and tread the path of VIRTUE, had grown a new hymen, and it was exceeding strong.

Thus did Fanny Hill triumph. She died a virgin!

IRA WALLACH

Blanche DuBois

(last seen being hustled off, at the instigation of Stanley Kowalski, to a mental institution in Tennessee Williams' A Streetcar Named Desire*)*

In the mental institution Blanche DuBois fell under the kindly ministrations of Dr. Pierre LeClerc, a masterful psychoanalyst and Creole cook, noted for his work in situational hysteria and jambalaya. Under his care, Blanche developed an avid interest in psychoanalysis. Dr. LeClerc encouraged her and guided her studies. When he declared her cured, she returned to New Orleans, where she hung out her shingle as a lay analyst. She was a strong believer in occupational therapy and she put all her patients to work making jambalaya.

Dr. LeClerc continued to take a paternal interest in her and it was he who, after a visit to her office, suggested that she market the many gallons of jambalaya now crowding her work space. She made a deal with a food distributor, arranged to have the product packaged and frozen, and marketed the product under the brand name, "Aunt Blanche's Jambalaya."

One day a new patient called on her. It was Stanley Kowalski. Because of what he had done to Blanche, Stanley was suffering from guilt feelings so severe that he was no longer functioning effectively at work. Never one to hold grudges, Blanche willingly forgot the past and set about helping Stanley. Within one year, Stanley's jambalaya was every bit as good as Dr. LeClerc's.

Blanche's career peaked when she was awarded two Cordons Bleu, one for her jambalaya, and one for her work in analysis.

IRA WALLACH

Kane and Shane

(last seen in the film High Noon *and in the film and novel* Shane *by Jack Schafer)*

As we left Shane, he was riding into "the heart of the great glowing West . . . whence he had come," having first taken care of some no-good skunks who were driving hapless homesteaders from their land . . . Shane, the ex-gunfighter, faster than lightning; Shane, the man who now sought peace, but whose quest was denied him by the no-good skunks.

And the last we saw of Will Kane, he had tossed his marshal's badge in the dust of the prairie town, showing his opinion of the cowardly townsfolk who refused to help him fight Frank Miller's bunch. Then he and Amy got into their buckboard and drove away.

But now we know what happened to them, thanks to some yellowed pioneer memoirs found in an old trunk near Busted Bedsprings, Texas.

Settling down, Will and Amy bought a store and Will became a peaceful "ribbon clerk." There, somewhere west of the Pecos and east of Eden, they were happy—for a while.

But one day a dark shadow fell athwart this scene, just as Shane came riding along. Feeling thirsty on this steaming hot day, he decided to stop and wet his whistle at a local saloon. But he was halted by a tobacco-stained old-timer. (Every Western town had one licensed TSOT.)

"Looks to me," said this worthy, "as if they's a mite of a ruckus over t' the gin'rl store."

Moseying over that way, Shane saw six hardbitten ruffians holding under their guns the lanky storekeeper and his pretty blond wife. While one scoundrel rifled the cash register, others wrecked canned goods, smashed open the cracker barrel, spilled beans, and tilted the pinball machine. One drunken lout wore a woman's beribboned hat as he pranced clownishly.

"I hate to say this, Amy," said Will Kane, "but it looks like they got us outnumbered three to one."

"Oh, Will!" sobbed Amy.

Shane spoke quietly: "Let these people go," he said. As no one heard him, he cleared his throat and tried again: "I SAID LET THESE PEOPLE GO!"

Silence fell. The swarthy leader scowled. "I'll be consarned and hornswoggled ef'n they aint some tight-pants little sissy a-giving us orders! Take keer of him, boys."

With lightning speed, two .45 Colts appeared as though from nowhere. One by one the ruffians fell.

Blam! Blam! Blam! Blam! Blam! Blam!

When it was over, Amy Kane blew the smoke from the muzzles of the twin Colts she had kept concealed in the folds of her gingham dress.

"That was some shootin', Amy" said Will Kane.

"We Girl Scouts are always prepared," said Amy calmly.

"What can I do for you, stranger?" Will asked, stepping over a corpse.

"I'd like to toast the little lady with a bottle of strawberry pop," said Shane. "Join me?"

"Don't mind if I do."

And so began one of the most enduring friendships the West had known. It lasted until a quarter after five the next Saturday.

ROBERT ALDRICH

Hans Castorp

(last seen in Thomas Mann's The Magic Mountain*)*

Hans Castorp served in the army of Kaiser Wilhelm with distinction. He received the Iron Cross for valor. After the war he was asked in a newspaper interview how he had remained so spectacularly cool under fire.

"No problem," said Castorp. "First of all, after all that endless conversation in the sanatorium, shellfire was like a lullaby. Humanism, absolutism, hedonism . . . who needs it? Plus that 'magic mountain' was full of crazies. Two of them fought a duel in which one of them shot himself. Deliberately! When you've seen something like that, you've seen it all."

When asked if he had any good prewar memories, Castorp produced a photograph. It was the X-ray plate of his friend Clavdia's chest. "We lost touch during the war," he said. "But I'm looking for her." He tapped the plate. "I'd know this anywhere."

Alice Adams

(last seen in Booth Tarkington's novel)

Alice's father Vergil ran an unsuccessful glue factory and Alice was a social climber who "put on airs" and turned suitors off. When we left the Adams family, Vergil was broke and Alice was resigned to attending secretarial school.

What happened thereafter is extracted from Alice's unpublished diary.

In the closing days of the operation of Vergil Adams' glue factory, Vergil was so upset that he was careless about quality control. What the heck, he thought, he was through anyhow. He took home a few cases of glue to store in his garage as mementos.

But one day, Vergil went out to his garage to glue a broken picture frame. The stuff dried almost before he could put the two pieces of the frame together at a correct angle. Plus Vergil's thumb and forefinger were glued to the frame.

He had discovered a forerunner of Krazy Glue! He sold the formula to a big glue company which paid him a huge sum just to keep it off the market.

Alice quit secretarial school and started putting on airs again. But this time everyone thought she was cute because she was rich.

Silas Marner

(last seen in George Eliot's novel)

We interviewed Hepzibah Marner Winthrop Gumm, the granddaughter of Eppie and Aaron Winthrop. "Grandma told lovely stories about old Silas Marner," she said. "He wasn't actually stingy. Just prudent. And really very generous. He gave Eppie a trousseau of bed linens he had woven himself, with gold coins in the hems! It was the earliest instance of mad money.

"Silas was a whiz of a weaver. Not many people knew that he expanded. He just wouldn't invest in publicity. The Marner Linen Mills are still going strong, though now it's all polyester."

Hepzibah's dream is for *Silas Marner* to become a PBS series. "So many generations of schoolchildren have been required to read about great-grandfather," she said, "and were completely turned off. A miniseries would take the stink off *Silas Marner*. Look what it did for the Forsytes."

Hepzibah is represented by Scott Meredith, who is rumored to be negotiating a seven-figure deal with the BBC.

Casanova

Giovanni Jacopo Casanova de Seingalt finished his memoirs in 1773. He died in 1798. What happened in those final twenty-five years is recorded in a journal packaged in a brown wrapper found recently in a second-hand shop in Barcelona.

What happened was that Casanova came to America at the suggestion of his friend Voltaire. Here he discovered the colonial custom of "bundling" and incorporated it into a dating service—the world's first.

The Revolution came along and ruined Casanova's business, so he began to practice another of his specialties: magic.

In Paris, he had done well by trying to produce a sex change by sorcery. But in Salem he was badly singed for his pains, and fled to Philadelphia, where he became a doctor in the Continental Army, specializing in gynecology.

Casanova catalogued his conquests only by initials—so we can only surmise who M.W., B.R., were. (Martha Washington?) (Betsy Ross?) But Casanova moved strictly in the upper crust.

Casanova left America at the same time that an army payroll disappeared. In his journal he complains bitterly about the exchange rate for Continental currency.

Kate

(last seen knuckling under to Petruchio in Shakespeare's The Taming of the Shrew*)*

Kate's transformation from shrew to doting housewife was no transitory phenomenon. For years she catered to her husband Petruchio's every whim, indulged his every caprice. She bore him eleven children—one a year—and their presence in the house made no contribution to gracious living. As infants, all the children regurgitated incessantly and this, too, affected the quality of life.

Except for Mario, who ran away from home at the age of twelve, Kate disliked her children intensely. When they approached her, their little arms outstretched as they begged for her love, she would say, "You want me to love you? Run away from home." Kate never revealed her dislike of the children to Petruchio. She never knew how much he hated those kids.

Petruchio, meanwhile, spent most of his time drinking away Kate's dowry.

As the years passed, Kate grew fatter and fatter and the faint mustache on her upper lip always glistened with sweat.

Then, in the fourteenth year of their marriage, Petruchio visited his friendly neighborhood apothecary and bought a vial of poison with which he spiked Kate's chianti. After she drank it down, Petruchio cried, "Die, woman, die!"

Ever obedient, Kate did as she was told.

Petruchio's act went unpunished because in those days wife-poisoning had been decriminalized.

Kate's funeral was a merry affair.

Ira Wallach

Leopold Bloom

(last seen in James Joyce's Ulysses*)*

Leopold Bloom was interviewed some years ago in his Dublin travel agency, which he had opened after he had taken the pledge. "After that June 16," he confided, "I went cold turkey. I decided to take it more than one day at a time."

Bloom looked remarkably fit for a man of his age. He attributed it to his diet of fried kidneys, hencod's roes, and the inner organs of beasts and fowls. What about cholesterol? Bloom had never heard of it.

He was philosphical about the past. Blazes Boylan was gone, killed in the Easter Monday uprising. Lenehan had died in the fighting; so had Joe Hynes and Paddy Dignam's son. The Citizen had died along with the drunkard, Bob Doran. Barney Kiernan's had closed.

And that young poet, Stephen Dedalus? "Ah, yes, the bullock befriending bard." Bloom smiled. "Young Dedalus, son of Simon Dedalus, had eloped to the continent with a pretty red-haired chambermaid, changed his name to James Joyce, wrote an account of all that happened to me on June 16, 1904. My interior monologue. How Molly had laughed when she read the book in Gibraltar. Yes, she was living there, watching the Barbary apes. She may come back to Dublin. A new night club is opening. The Don Giovanni. It would like her.

"Dedalus was brilliant," he said warmly. "He made it possible for me to appreciate my subconscious."

JOHN FERRIS

Jeeves

(last seen in the novels of P.G. Wodehouse)

One might suppose that after lifting his last silver salver bearing a weekend invitation to Twing Hall, or perhaps a lemon-squash pick-me-up, Jeeves would retire to the Old Butler's Home in the Cotswolds. Far from it. Bertie Wooster has broken silence to tell all:

It was one of those mornings when I awoke feeling strangely depressed, with a strong feeling of loss, as though someone near and dear had slipped over the brink. In fact, I felt rather like that Scandinavian chap Shakespeare wrote about, the one who was always asking himself why he should hang about any longer. "That is the question," the fellow used to say, juggling somebody's skull, as I recall. Gloomy sort.

"You rang, sir?" The apparition that drifted into my bedroom was called George or Algernon, something like that. As I struggled to remember the bloke's name, I suddenly knew what had brought on the black fits. Jeeves was no longer at my beck, nor even my call.

"George—" I began.

"John, if you please, sir," the bloke corrected me.

"John, pack my bag at once. I'm off to look up old Jeeves."

Poor Jeeves; probably spending his days by the chimney fire, having his broth spooned up by some ancient of a nurse.

I spilled off the crowded bus at this tiny seaside town and tottered up to the High Street. I was nearly knocked over by one of those jogging chaps in shorts and cap with an enormous tassel. Rather an elderly duffer. "Look here—!" I shouted at him, and then, as we stared at each other, recognition dawned like one of those Technicolor sunrises you see in the cinema, when the music swells.

"Jeeves!" I cried. "Can it be you?"

"Indeed, sir. Pleasure to see you." He was hardly breathing.

"What the devil are you up to?"

"My morning ten-mile run, sir. I find it tones up the liver, brings on the ruddy cheek. You ought to try it, sir. You're looking a big peaked, if I may say so."

"Never mind that, Jeeves. I thought I'd find you in a wheelchair or at least wobbling about on a cane or two, not dashing around like one of those chaps in *Chariots of Fire*."

"I am happy to say, sir, that a lifelong regimen of exercise and sound nutrition has resulted in a fair degree of good health."

"The point is, Jeeves—"

But that was a statement that remained unfinished as Jeeves seized me and shoved me roughly against the side of a building, while jabbing an elbow somewhere between my third and fourth vertebra.

"Jeeves, what the deuce!" I cried, gasping for air.

"Beg pardon, sir, but it was necessary to dislodge you from your position to avoid being seen. I fear you are being followed."

"Followed. Who, me?" I couldn't have been more startled had Jeeves broken into a chorus of "Over the Rainbow" while accompanying himself on the zither and dancing the hornpipe.

"Exactly, sir," said Jeeves. "I took the liberty of dropping your name while on a mission to Bucharest. You see, whilst on an assignment behind the Iron Curtain, I found myself in a jam, to employ an American expression. In a weak moment, I supplied your name in place on my own. You have been, I think the term is, 'shadowed' ever since."

"But what were you doing there?"

"Disguised in the role of an ambassador's gentleman, sir, I managed to secure some highly valuable information regarding missile defenses, with the aid of a young lady of doubtful reputation. That information, sir, is now concealed inside a sesame bun in that hamburger emporium across the street."

I saw it now. Poor old Jeeves had slipped around the corner. Gone off his rocker. Turned dotty in his dotage. I decided to humor him. "Of course," I said. "Now the job is to get the information to the proper authorities."

"Precisely, sir. I marvel at your perspicacity. We shall wait here till your pursuer gives up, then signal my confederate to send the bun on its way to MI-5."

I was pondering where the old fellow might be sent for medical assistance when a large man in a bowler hat approached us.

"Well done, 008," he said to Jeeves. "We've copped your shadow and the bun is off to London. Good work. Now who's this blighter?" he demanded, twisting my arm. "Tried to mug you, eh? Come on, chappie, it's off to the cooler for you."

Jeeves intervened. "Control, may I introduce Mr. Wooster. And may I add, his aid has been invaluable."

When he left, I said, "Jeeves, have you gone starko? This is nonsense!"

"Of course it is, sir," said Jeeves. "You see, when I stopped working in Mr. Wodehouse's novels, I began working in thrillers. Novels of suspense, they call them. Espionage, intrigue. I'll admit it is pretty silly. But it's a living."

I felt better knowing that Jeeves was sane. We went across the street to the hamburger heaven and shared a moody pot of tea, brewed from a tea bag.

"I say, Jeeves," I said, "do you think there might be something to do for me in these . . . thrillers?"

"I'll certainly look into it, sir," said Jeeves. "But I very much doubt it. Thrillers don't have gentlemen in them. But as Psmith used to say: You never can tell."

ROBERT ALDRICH

RYE
TO NEW YORK
FROM N

Missing Personae

Do you know the whereabouts of a fictional character? Enter the "Whatever Happened To . . ." Contest by supplying the further adventures of a fictional character of your acquaintance. The author of the entry judged by Andrews, McMeel & Parker to be the best will win $1,000. The rules are simple:

1) Entries may be of any length and entrants may submit more than one entry, but each entry should be typewritten, double spaced, on a single sheet of paper. Each entry should be clearly labeled with the entrant's name, address, and phone number. Entries will be judged solely on the basis of originality and creativity. Employees of Universal Press Syndicate, Universal Licensing Corporation, Andrews, McMeel & Parker and their families are ineligible.

2) All entries must be original and previously unpublished. Submission to the contest grants us the right to publish the material, with proper credit, in exchange for Andrews, McMeel & Parker's consideration of the entry.

3) The deadline is December 31, 1985. The award winner will be announced in a press release by March 31, 1986.

Send your entries to:

"WHATEVER HAPPENED TO . . ." CONTEST
Andrews, McMeel & Parker
4400 Johnson Drive
Fairway, Kansas 66205